It's fun to draw **H**orses, **P**onies, and **F**arm **A**nimals

It's fun to draw
Horses, Ponies, and Farm Animals

Mark Bergin

Sky Pony Press
New York

HOW TO USE THIS BOOK:
Start by following the numbered splats on the lefthand page. These steps will ask you to add some lines to your drawing. The new lines are always drawn in red so you can see how the drawing builds from step to step. Read the "You can do it!" splats to learn about drawing and shading techniques you can use.

Sky Pony Press books may be purchased in bulk at special discounts for sales promotion, corporate gifts, fund-raising, or educational purposes. Special editions can also be created to specifications. For details, contact the Special Sales Department, Sky Pony Press, 307 West 36th Street, 11th Floor, New York, NY 10018 or info@ skyhorsepublishing.com.

Sky Pony® is a registered trademark of Skyhorse Publishing, Inc.®, a Delaware corporation.

Visit our website at www.skyponypress.com.

10 9 8 7 6 5 4 3

This product conforms to CPSIA 2008

Library of Congress Cataloging-in-Publication Data on file.

Cover design by Michael Short
Cover illustration by Mark Bergin

ISBN: 978-1-5107-4146-1

Printed in the United States of America

Contents

Contents

It's fun to draw

Horses, Ponies, and Farm Animals

Rearing horse

1 Start by drawing a bean shape for the body.

2 Draw in the legs and hooves.

splat-a-fact
A male horse is called a stallion.

you can do it!
Use a felt-tip marker for the lines then add color using crayons.

3 Draw in the head, mouth, neck, and tail.

4 Draw in the ears and mane. Add dots for the eye and nostrils.

8

Rodeo horse

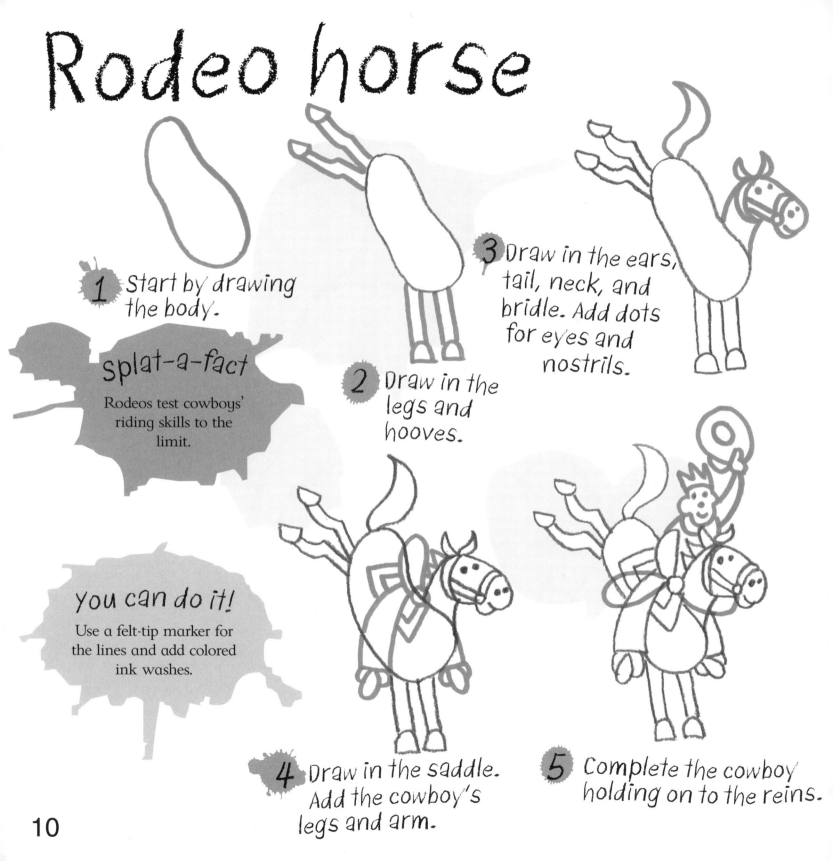

1 Start by drawing the body.

Splat-a-fact

Rodeos test cowboys' riding skills to the limit.

2 Draw in the legs and hooves.

3 Draw in the ears, tail, neck, and bridle. Add dots for eyes and nostrils.

you can do it!

Use a felt-tip marker for the lines and add colored ink washes.

4 Draw in the saddle. Add the cowboy's legs and arm.

5 Complete the cowboy holding on to the reins.

Shire horse

1 Start by drawing a bean shape for the body.

2 Draw in four legs.

3 Draw in the head, ears, neck, and tail. Add the harness.

Splat-a-fact

Shire horses are one of the largest horse breeds.

you can do it!

Use felt-tip marker for the lines. Color in with colored crayons and blend with your fingers.

4 Draw in the face and bridle details. Add a plow and a line for the field.

5 Draw in the farmer.

Horse's head

1 Start by cutting out the shape of the head and neck. Glue down.

splat-a-fact
Horses love to eat hay.

2 Cut out the ears and glue down. Draw in the eyes, nostrils, and mouth.

you can do it!
Cut out the shapes from colored paper and glue in place. Use a felt-tip marker for details.

3 Cut out the brown mane and white nose patch. Glue down.

Galloping horse

1 Start with a bean shape for the body.

2 Draw in the head, neck, and tail.

you can do it!

Use a felt-tip marker for the lines. Use crayons for detail then paint on top—the wax will act as a resistant.

splat-a-fact

Horses are herbivores (plant eaters).

3 Draw in the legs and hooves.

4 Add the markings, mane, eye, nostril, and mouth.

Dressage

1 Start by drawing a bean shape for the body.

2 Draw in the legs and hooves. Add a line for the ground.

you can do it!

Use a black felt-tip marker for the lines. Color in with colored felt-tip markers.

3 Draw in the blanket, tail, and head. Add the bridle and a dot for the eye.

4 Draw in the ear and mane. Add a rider, saddle, and the reins.

Shetland pony

1 Start by drawing a bean shape for the body.

2 Draw in the legs and hooves.

you can do it!
Use a felt-tip marker for the lines and add color using colored oil pastels.

splat-a-fact
Shetland ponies are small and are often ridden by children.

3 Add a tail and grass.

4 Draw in the head details and long mane.

Racing horse

1 Start by drawing a bean shape for the body.

2 Draw in the legs and hooves.

Splat-a-fact
Horce racing has been practiced since ancient times.

You can do it!
Use a felt-tip marker for the lines and add color using chalk pastels.

3 Draw in the head and blinker hood. Add the neck, saddle, blanket, and tail.

4 Draw in the jockey holding on to the reins.

Pony family

1 Start by drawing two overlapping bean shapes.

2 Draw in the ponies' legs and hooves. Add the ground line.

you can do it!

Draw the lines with a felt-tip marker and use torn tissue paper for color.

Splat-a-fact

Foals learn to stand within an hour of being born.

3 Draw in two heads and necks.

4 Add the face details, ears, manes, and tails.

24

Stable

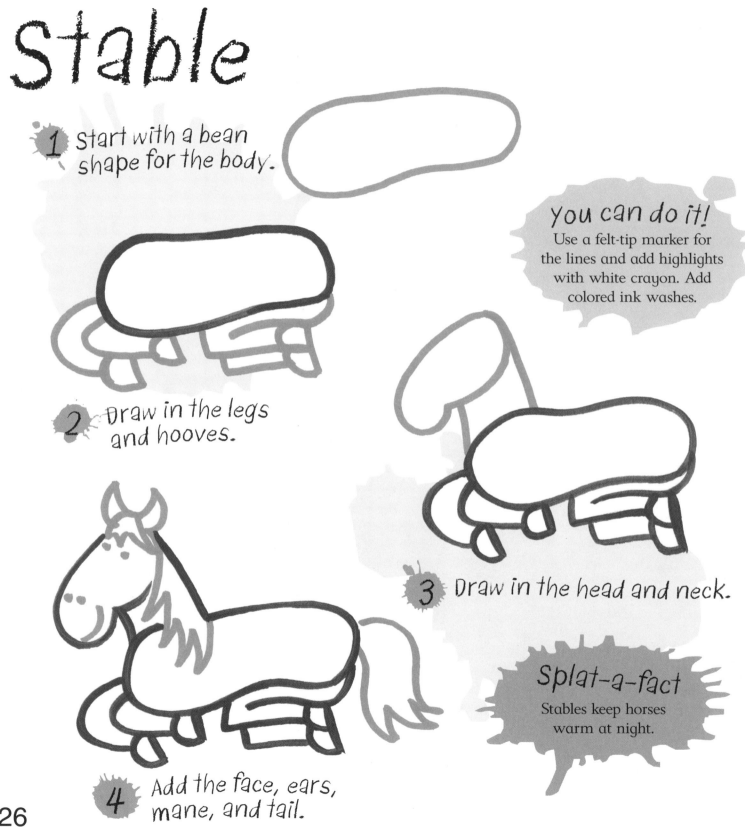

1 Start with a bean shape for the body.

2 Draw in the legs and hooves.

3 Draw in the head and neck.

4 Add the face, ears, mane, and tail.

you can do it!
Use a felt-tip marker for the lines and add highlights with white crayon. Add colored ink washes.

Splat-a-fact
Stables keep horses warm at night.

Military horse

you can do it!
Use a felt-tip marker for the lines and color in with colored pencils.

1 Start with a bean shape for the body.

2 Draw in the legs and hooves.

Splat-a-fact
Horses have been used in warfare for over 5,000 years.

3 Draw in the head, neck, and tail. Add the face and ears, then the bridle and saddle.

4 Draw in the soldier holding his sword.

28

Rolling horse

1 Start with a bean shape for the body.

2 Draw in the legs and hooves.

splat-a-fact
Sometimes horses roll on the ground to stretch their muscles.

you can do it!
Use a felt-tip marker for the lines and then add color with watercolor paints. Dab on more color with a sponge for added texture.

3 Draw in the neck and head.

4 Draw in the face details and ears. Add the mane and tail.

Polo horse

1 Start by drawing a bean shape for the body.

2 Draw in the legs and hooves.

you can do it!

Use a felt-tip marker for the lines. Use colored pencils to color in. Place paper on a bumpy surface to add texture.

splat-a-fact

A polo team has four players.

3 Draw in the head, face, and bridle. Add the tail and saddle.

4 Draw in the polo player with a stick and ball.

Show jumping

1 Start with a bean shape for the body.

2 Draw in the legs and hooves. Add a tail.

you can do it!

Use a felt-tip marker for the lines and add scribble textures with crayon. Paint over with a watercolor wash.

splat-a-fact

A show jumping course consists of different obstacles to jump over.

3 Draw in the head, neck, bridle, and saddle blanket.

4 Draw in the rider holding the reins. Add the saddle.

Chicken

1 Start with the head. Add a dot for the eye.

2 Add the beak and head details.

3 Add the body.

4 Draw in a wing and tail feathers.

you can do it!

Use oil pastels and smudge them with your finger. Use a felt-tip marker for the lines.

splat-a-fact

Male chickens are larger and more brightly colored than females.

5 Draw in two legs and feet.

Cow

1 Start with the head and add two rounded shapes.

2 Add the eyes, nostrils, ears, and horns.

3 Draw in the body.

4 Add four legs and hooves.

5 Draw in a tail, udder, and markings. Add grass.

You can do it!

Use crayons for texture and paint over with watercolor paint. Use a felt-tip marker for the lines.

38

splat-a-fact

No two cows have the same markings or spots.

Donkey

1 Draw a bean shape with a dot for the eye.

2 Add nostrils and a mouth.

3 Add ears, a neck, and a mane.

4 Draw in a curved body and a tail.

5 Add four legs and hooves.

you can do it!

Use a black felt-tip marker for the lines and add color using colored felt-tip markers.

Mallard

you can do it!

Use oil pastels and smudge them with your finger. Use a felt-tip marker for the lines.

1 Start with the head and add a dot for the eye.

2 Draw in the beak.

splat-a-fact

Mallards have webbed feet designed for swimming.

3 Draw in the body with a pointed tail. Add a curved line for the wing and across the chest.

4 Add legs with webbed feet and a zig-zag line around the neck.

43

Farm cat

1 Start by drawing a furry body and head shape.

2 Add another ear, an eye, nose, and whiskers.

3 Add furry legs and paws. Draw a triangle shape inside the ear.

splat-a-fact

Cats have very good night vision.

4 Draw in a bushy tail. Add a striped pattern.

44

Goat

1 Start with the head.

2 Draw in ears, eyes, and a nose.

3 Add two horns, a neck, and a beard.

splat-a-fact

Goats have four stomachs.

4 Draw in the body and tail.

you can do it!

Use crayons for all textures and paint over with watercolor paint. Use a blue felt-tip marker for the lines.

5 Add the legs and hooves.

47

Duck

1 Start with the body shape and tail feathers.

2 Add the beak.

3 Draw in two webbed feet.

4 Add eyes and a wing. Finish with the beak details.

you can do it!
Use colored pencils and a felt-tip marker for the lines. Use pencils in a scribbly way so the color looks more interesting.

Owl

1 Start with the head shape. Add a curved line for detail.

2 Draw in the eyes and a beak.

you can do it!
Tear up colored tissue paper and glue it down for the color. Use a felt-tip marker for the lines.

3 Draw the body shape and a fan-shaped tail.

4 Add two large pointed wings.

5 Add two legs and feet.

Splat-a-fact
Barn owls do not hoot— they screech!

50

51

Pig

1 Start with the head. Add an oval for the nose.

2 Add the ears, eyes, nostrils, and a mouth.

3 Add the body.

4 Draw in a curly tail and add spotted markings.

5 Add four legs and feet.

Splat-a-fact

Some pigs have tusks to fight with and dig for food.

52

Rabbit

1. Start with a circle for the head and an oval for the body.

2. Add the eyes, teeth, a nose, mouth, and whiskers.

you can do it!
Draw in the lines with a brown felt-tip marker. Use colored pencils to add color.

3. Add four legs.

4. Add a tail and ears.

Splat-a-fact
There are about 25 different species of rabbit.

Sheep

1 Start with a fluffy body.

2 Draw in the head shape with a fluffy top and add ears.

3 Draw two dots for eyes, nostrils, and grass.

4 Draw in four legs and feet and add a tail.

you can do it!
Use watercolor paint to color. Use a sponge to dab on the paint for added texture.

Sheepdog

splat-a-fact

Sheepdogs help farmers to round up sheep.

1 Start by cutting out the shape of the body.

2 Cut out another furry shape and glue down.

3 Draw in the eyes, nose, tongue, and outline.

you can do it!
Cut the shapes out of colored paper and glue in place. The dog's head must overlap the body.

4 Cut out more fur for the head and glue down.

58

Turkey

1 Start with a big curl to make an oval-shaped body.

2 Add fan-shaped feathers.

3 Draw two legs and spiky feet.

Splat-a-fact

A baby turkey is called a poult.

4 Draw in a neck and head. Add a beak and a dot for the eye. Add head details and zig-zag lines for the tail feathers.

About the Author

Mark Bergin was born in Hastings, England. He has illustrated an award-winning series and written over twenty books. He has done many book designs, layouts, and storyboards in many styles, including cartoons for numerous books, posters, and advertisements. He lives in Bexhill-on-Sea with his wife and three children.

Index